Copyright © 2013 by Hispanic Economics, Inc.

Manufactured in the United States of America. All rights reserved. No part of this book may be reproduced in any form or by any means, electronic or mechanical, including photocopying, recording, or by information storage and retrieval systems—except by a reviewer who may quote brief passages in a review to be printed in a magazine, newspaper, or on the Web—without permission in writing from the publisher. This book is presented solely for educational and entertainment purposes. All the opinions expressed are those of the author and do not reflect those of Hispanic Economics, Inc., its employees or clients. Although the author and publisher have made every effort to ensure that the information in this book was correct at press time, the author and publisher do not assume and hereby disclaim any liability to any party for any loss, damage, or disruption caused by errors or omissions, whether such errors or omissions result from negligence, accident, or any other cause.

First printing 2013

Publication date: April 2013

ATTENTION CORPORATIONS, UNIVERSITIES, COLLEGES, AND PROFESSIONAL AND CHARITABLE ORGANIZATIONS: Quantity discounts are available on bulk purchases of this book for educational and gift purposes, or as premiums in fundraising efforts. Inquiries should be sent to info@hispaniceconomics.com.

>   Hispanic Economics, Inc.
>   P.O. Box 140681
>   Coral Gables, FL 33114-0681
>   info@hispaniceconomics.com
>   HispanicEconomics.com

ISBN 978-1-9398790-1-1

All photographs are by the author, except for the following: Mathieu Brees (page 46); Colin Cooke (pages 26 and 28); Ron Cooper (page 27); Aram Dulgarian (page 60); Gustavo Estrada (pages 15 and 25); and Stephen Myers (pages 24, 40, 49, 50, 52, 53, 54, 56, 63 and 66).

Cover and Interior Design by John Clifton
john@johnclifton.net

The publisher is grateful to Stephen Myers for providing cocktail recipes and other mixed drink recipes included in this book; each individual mixologist is acknowledged. As with any alcoholic product, excessive drinking can cause serious physical harm. Please enjoy mezcal responsibly.

This book is for María Varela Petersen

About the Author

Louis E.V. Nevaer is a leading authority on the three great flavors of southern Mexico: mezcal, chocolate, and coffee. He divides his time between New York and Mexico, with no regrets.

Contents

No Mezcal Is Illegal   7

Move Over Tequila, Mezcal Has Arrived   10

The Making of the Perfect Wonder   13

Tequila Paves the Way   16

Mezcal—The Linguistic Origin   17

The Geography of Mezcal Dreams   18

Women of Mezcal—Mezcalilleras   23

The Bearers of Firewater   26

Mezcal in Oaxaca City   31

The Mezcal in Your Spa   41

The Camino Unreal   42

Medicinal Mezcal   44

Sexual Mezcal   45

Mezcal, Coffee & Chocolate—The Palate of Indulgence   48

A Marriage Made in Mexico   50

Mezcal in the Kitchen   52

Mezcal Drinks   56

Mezcal Roads   68

No Mezcal is Illegal

Some may be undocumented. Others may lack pedigree. But no mezcal is alien to the palate of humanity.

And while mezcal is not as famous as tequila, there lies its appeal. It is an artisanal elixir, enjoyed in the quiet gatherings of friends, the raucous celebrations of mountain villages, the contemplative offerings to the gods.

Mezcal has a history that goes back more than half a millennium, older than tequila. The grandfather of agave spirits, mezcal is a state of anticipation. It reflects the indigenous sensibilities of the peoples of Mexico and the technical expertise of European immigrants. The Spanish introduced distillation to Mexico in the early 1500s. Before then, the Maya, Mixtec, and Zapotec peoples used agave to make a beer-like beverage that contained 3 percent alcoholic content.

It was technological innovation that made mezcal as we know it today possible. And it is the variety of agave plants from which mezcal can be made that allows for its exuberant variety. Whereas tequila can only be made from 100 percent blue agave, mezcal can be made from one of 25 recognized agave varieties, provided they are harvested from specific regions of Mexico. Mezcal is only mezcal if the agave comes from one of five states in southern Mexico, with Oaxaca being the principal source.

Most artisans use a blend of agaves, with agave espandin being the preferred choice. The use of various agaves, however, allows each distiller to create a signature product, with its own unique scent and taste.

The two other characteristics that distinguish mezcal from tequila are derived from the distillation process and the artisanal nature of the final product. Whereas tequila is steam cooked and distilled in column stills, mezcal is roasted in wood-fired pits and distilled in small batches using copper stills. And while tequila is only required to use 51 percent agave spirits (and may be bottled anywhere), mezcal must contain

100 percent agave (and be bottled at the source). Mezcal has its own Domination of Origin Status and certification, which is not the case with tequila.

That mezcal comes from the south of Mexico also allows it to be paired with two other delicacies associated with southern Mexico: robust coffee and delectable chocolates.

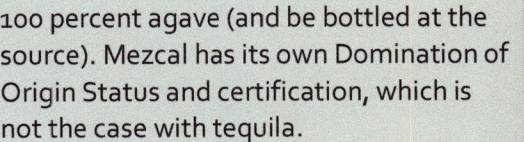

Mezcal Has Arrived

Move Over Tequila

Yes, you and I both know that tequila and mezcal are related, since they are both made from the agave plant.

Ah, the agave plant, the century plant to you, gentle reader of English.

Tequila and mezcal, these Mexican spirits, are brothers, born of the same mother.

Tequila is known around the world as the drink of Mexico. But what of mezcal? What is mezcal known for?

Mezcal is the soul of Mexico. Mezcal is the connoisseur's ecstasy of Mexico.

Mezcal is the essence of modern Mexico. It exists only because miscegenation exists. The pre-Hispanic fermentation that created pulque combines with the post-Hispanic passion for distillation. The two intermarried and combined, like lovers wrapped around each other, and produced mezcal, the firewater flowing from their naked bodies.

This was the in the 16th century, and for more than 400 years, mezcal has been engraved in Mexico's soul, an essential element of the Mexican palate.

Yet, until recently, mezcal was hidden from the world.

That may be its saving grace: its purity lies in its splendid isolation, its unadulterated pedigree, its loneliness that speaks of the human condition, its ability to lead you to the conclusion of a world of existential ambivalence.

Fine mezcals are made by Oaxacan villagers scattered in scores of towns and villages throughout this southern Mexican state. Created through centuries-old traditions, mezcal is made by villagers, each specific mezcal reflecting the elements of its environment and the unique methods each *mezcalero* uses in the creation of this spirit.

So, now, then: picture it!

It is early morning and you are in Oaxaca. Your memory is hazy. You don't immediately recognize the room, with its 20-foot ceilings and stone walls, that was built as a convent, but now has 24-hour room service. By the floor lie two empty bottles of mezcal, glassware, and what resembles the remains of a banana split.

Oh, yes, and the phone rings and it's the concierge, reminding you that the prescription the doctor gave you last night has been delivered to the front desk. Why is this happening? What does this mean? Is this the normal state of affairs at the Camino Real in Oaxaca City?

You will definitely ask yourself, *How did I end up here?*

The last thing you might remember is that you embarked on a journey of discovery, making pilgrimages to the *mezcaleteras* of Oaxaca City the night before.

Think of these as temples to mezcal. Think of them as temples, period.

The agave plant rivals the Virgin of Guadalupe in the popular imagination. A ubiquitous Mexican skull sculpture rests next to a flask of an unnamed mezcal, unnamed because no one has bothered to give it a name, it is that artisanal.

We need to backtrack.

Yes, that's a sensible approach. If we are to understand the set of events that led you to wake up in the Camino Real Oaxaca, with a room service tray littered with glassware and the remains of a banana split, surrounded by bottles of mezcal . . .

Yes, backtrack, rewind time, move in reverse . . . take the mezcal and trace it back to the agave plant from which it came . . .

The Making of the Perfect Wonder

Mezcal . . . a word that refers to a kind of *aguaridente*, Spanish for firewater, a spirit distilled from the agave plant. And the agave plant is related to the maguey, the century plant . . . which was used to make pulque, a potent beverage used in pre-Hispanic Mexico as an offering to the gods.

First, recall: mezcal is distilled from the crushed, roasted hearts of the agave. It is an artisanal spirit, one that reflects the various, nuanced traditions of the First Peoples who populated the sierras of Mexico. It also reflects the distillation techniques that the Spanish introduced from Europe beginning in the 16th century, where "country" spirits, such as the grappes and slivovitzes, are common.

In Mexico, the production of mezcal consists of these Ten Commanding steps:

1. Spiked leaves of the agave are harvested prior to the plant flowering. It is during this time that the sugar content is highest. It is now, as the agave is about to flower, that the hearts become engorged with honey water—*agua miel*—and they swell in size.

2. The heart of the agave is pried from the ground, and the leaves and shoots are cut off and discarded.

3. The hearts resemble large pineapples and are called *piñas*, Spanish for pineapples.

4. The *piñas* are gathered and brought to the *palenque*, the place where mezcal is produced. This is usually on a property adjacent to a family dwelling, since much of mezcal production continues to be artisanal, a cottage industry.

5. The *piñas* are roasted in an earthen oven pit, usually lined with rocks that have been heated by a bonfire; the stones are ready when they are white-hot.

6. The hearts are roasted, usually whole, by being left in the pit, covered with the leaves or fiber of the maguey, at least overnight but usually until the pit cools, which can be a day or longer. It is this underground cooking process that suffuses mezcal with its distinctive smokiness.

7. The hearts are removed from the pit and then crushed in a circular millstone, known as a *tahona*, often pulled by horse or donkey, and the result is mixed with water and gathered in a vat, where it ferments. This fermentation process can take anywhere from three to six days, depending on the artisan, the climate, and the judgment of the artisan.

8. The mash is then distilled in copper or clay alembics, often several times, and the result is a clear liquid— *punta*—which is distilled again to become the Perfect Wonder: Mezcal.

9. It is now that the mezcal is aged in barrels. The longer it ages, the more it acquires the scent of the oak barrels as it mellows, becoming like a fine cognac.

10. The aging process determines whether it is *añejo* (aged briefly) or *reposado* (aged for more time).

This is the ten-step process by which redemption is delivered to humanity. Rumor has it that it was delivered to humanity by Charlton Heston's ancestor on two tablets when he descended from the Madre Sierra Occidental, or something along those lines. Or perhaps not.

But I digress.

And although some commercial manufacturers tend to blend several varieties of mezcal, most artisanal ones are made from a single still at one *palenque*. This is how mezcal best resembles a fine single malt scotch.

But I digress once more. How did mezcal, this perfect wonder, lead me to this state?

Tequila Paves the Way

Tequila is made from the blue agave plant that is cultivated in specific regions of Mexico. A generation ago tequila was dismissed by sophisticated Mexicans who looked to other countries for their fine spirits. In the homes of well-heeled Mexicans, one would be offered brandy or cognac or whiskey, but tequila?

¡*Que Dios nos ampare!* May God spare us!

Never.

That was then, of course. That was a generation ago, a generation before globalization forced the Mexicans to move beyond their self-loathing—so ingrained in their psyche it has its own word: *malinchismo*. Globalization forced the Mexicans to accept one undisputable fact: Mexico is home to some damn good things, second to none!

Now even doubting fools—*estos cabrones*—know better.

Today there are scores of excellent tequilas coveted around the globe, and there is a vibrant market throughout the world for Mexican spirits. Tequila has become its own category of liquor, made and marketed by large companies with enormous marketing budgets. Have you looked at the billboards, or the full-page advertisements in glossy magazines lately? Tequila is enjoyed by sophisticates the world over who demand nothing less than excellence.

What of mezcal, that distilled spirit made in lonely villages and towns across desert landscapes, by people who have never traveled the world?

Tequila paved the way for mezcal's ascendance in the world of refined spirits . . .

'Mezcal' – the Linguistic Origin

What, in this world, isn't in contention?

That said, Mexicans have reached a consensus on the origin of the word *mezcal*. It is derived from the Náhuatl words *metl* ("maguey") and *calli* ("cooked") and means "cooked maguey." Mezcal means three different things in Mexico. Throughout northern Mexico mezcal refers to the agave plant itself. Everywhere in Mexico, it is also the name for the spirit derived from the plant's fermented sap. To linguists and historians, the word denotes the cooked maguey stems and leaf basis, characterized by a high sugar content and associated with a spirit that enjoyed manifold cultural purposes in the lives of the First Peoples of the Mexican nation.

The Geography of Mezcal Dreams

1

It is not down on any map. It is down on every map. It is the geography of desire, the landscape of dreams to be fulfilled. This is Mexico, the Mexico where years pass like the pages of a book with several thousand leaves. It is the Mexico that defies description, but not storytelling.

It is a nation best envisioned first by narrative—epic tales—and visuals. Then, experienced through the senses, it becomes a sensual experience of sight and scent, sound and touch. And taste.

Although this account focuses on the artisanal mezcals produced in Oaxaca, the maguey plant is found throughout the country. The narrative begins with the geographical domains of where maguey flourishes, and where the agave species used to make mezcal are found: along the highways that wind through Mexico, the sierras, valleys, mountains, plateaus—littered with villages, histories, ghosts—and the deserts of longing.

There is desert and darkness. There are long stretches of road, through mountain valleys and across plateaus.
The deserts long for the rains, but the agave longs for nothing.
The years drift by, each one a link in the necklace of eternity, which ensnares and strangles lovers.
You find yourself driving, driving through the desert roads. You can feel propelled forward toward the unknown. The deserts stretch before you. So does the agave.
Mezcal. Mezcal calls you.
What are your secrets?
Mezcal knows your secrets. To whom can you confide your secrets?
Mezcal.
The mezcal knows your longing.
Mezcal calls you home.
Drink of the nectar that becomes agave. Reach for the agave.
The agave drains the moisture from the deserts, and its thorns point towards the darkness and the heavens.
The agave flourishes in the deserts where humanity withers.
The agave longs for nothing, not even the caress of humanity.
The great Mexican Sierras offer sustenance to the plant. There are villages where each mezcal is a signature creation, reflecting the essence of the place, the scent and flavors of the earth.
Mezcal. Mezcal calls out your name.
The deserts long for rains; humanity longs for sustenance.
Mezcal.
Its mother, the agave, longs for nothing.

- Mark Santiago

The agave species used in mezcal production thrive in arid climates, where there is little rain, high temperatures, and thin soil. The climate is temperate and the elevation ranges from 3,000 to 6,000 feet (1,000 to 2,000 meters) above sea level.

The combination of altitude, moisture, and soil determine the flavor and scent of the mezcals produced, meaning that there are distinct flavor profiles depending on the geography of each village. The maguey's natural environments range from deserts and scrublands to dry and temperate forests and arid plateaus across the western and southern Mexican landscapes. These regions have names, wonderful, lyrical names: Sierra Madre Occidental, Sierra Madre del Sur, and Sierra Nevada.

Which one calls your name?

Which one beckons you with the promise of a road trip?

I can see you in a convertible chasing the sunsets, with an irresistible paramour by your side and sidekicks in the back.

The human brain is estimated to have anywhere from 80 to 120 billion cells. I absolve you of any guilt you may have for killing a few million brain cells from a mezcal binge; it isn't as if you're using all of those brain cells, anyway. At least not in this lifetime.

Here is an overview of states other than Oaxaca where mezcal is distilled, with a description of the agaves used in each region.

Chiapas

The town of Comitlán is well known for its mezcal, made from maguey amarillo (*A. salmiana*).

Durango

The three towns best known for their mezcal are Mezquital, Nombre de Dios, and Tamazula, where the maguey cenizo (*A. durangensis*) and tepemate (*A. angustifolia*) are used. On occasion, masparillo (*A. bovicormuta* and *A. maximiliana*) is also used to make excellent mezcals, but this is rare and only occurs in villages in the southern part of the state.

Guerrero

The most well-known region for mezcal in Guerrero State is El Chilapan, where the towns of Ahuacuotzingo, Chilapa, Márti de Cuilapan, and Zitlala excel at producing fine spirits. Mezcals from Guerrero are usually made from the papalote (*A. cupreata*) species that grows along the Balsas River area, one of the few areas agave is cultivated amid forests, primarily oak forests here.

Jalisco

This is the land of tequila! Yet . . . mezcal is also found here. Blame or credit the town of Zapotitlán, which is known to produce about a dozen or so mezcals, primarily from the lechuguilla (*A. maximiliana*), maguey liñera (*A. angustifolio*) and ixtlero amarillo (*A. rhodacantha*) species. Other towns known for mezcal production include Tolimán, Tonaya, and Zapotitlán.

Michoacán

The towns best known for their mezcals include Erongarícuaro, Hidalgo, Indaparapeo, Madero, Morelia, Tacámbaro, and Tzitzio. Most are located off the Balsa River basin, located in the Sierra Madre del Sur. The two most popular agaves are the maguey chino (*A. cupreata*) and maguey largo (*A. inaequidens*).

Puebla

Three towns are renowned for their mezcals. One is Caltepec, where villagers make mezcal from papalometl (*A. potatorum*) and pitzometl (*A. marmorata*) agaves. Another town is Ixtacamaxtitlán, where villagers make mezcal from the maguey Amarillo (*A. salmiana* var. *salmiana*). And the third is Tepeojuma, where villagers use espadilla agave (*A. angustifolia*) to make mezcal.

San Luis Potosí-Zacatecas

The mezcal-producing region overlaps these two states into a single ecological area where the agave for spirits is located. Maguey verde (*A. salmiana* var. *crassipina*) is used by artisans to make mezcal. The towns best known for their mezcal are Shualulco, Charcas, Salinas, and Pinos. A claim to fame is that in the town of Teúl de González Ortega (Zacatecas State), villagers produce mezcal from the blue agave (*A. tequilana Weber*), which is almost otherwise exclusively used to make tequila.

Sonora

The regional mezcal is known as *bacanora* (made from *A. angustifolio* and *A. rhodacantha*). There is a cluster of villages and towns around the Sierra Madre Occidental that constitute the mezcal-producing region of the state. These towns include Bacanora, Baviácora, Huásabas, Moctezuma, and Nácori Chico. Other agave varieties are also used to make small quantities of mezcal from three agaves, lechuguilla (*A. shrevei*), lechuguilla de la sierra (*A. bovicormuta*), and mezcal ceniza (*A. colorata*).

Tamaulipas

In the San Carlos mountains, where the towns of Burgos, Cruillas, Jiménez, Méndez, San Nicolás, and San Carlos are located, mezcal, known locally as *vino* or *vino-mezcal*, has gained a strong following. Most of these mezcals are made from the maguey cenizo (*A. Americana* var. *protoamericana*) and jarcia (*A. motium-sancticaroli*). In the southwestern region of the state, the towns of Bustamente, Jaumave, Miquihuana, Palmillas, and Tula are gaining notoriety for their own artisanal mezcals.

Agaves of Oaxaca

All magueys, or agaves, belong to the Agavaceae family and are indigenous to the New World. They are found from as far north as Utah and Nevada in the United States and south to the northern areas of Colombia and Venezuela. They are also found throughout the Caribbean islands. More than 200 have been identified. One hundred fifty are found in Mexico, 104 of which are endemic to the Mexican nation.

There are 38 species of agave in Oaxaca State. Seventeen are cultivated to make mezcal, with Espadín (*A. angustifolia*) being the most widely used agave. This is the agave that one finds cultivated in the areas of Ejutla, Miahuatlán, Ocotlán, Tlacolula, Sola de Vega, Yautepec, and Zimatlán.

The other agave species harvested throughout Oaxaca for mezcal are:

- Arroqueño (*A. americana* var. *americana*)
- Cirial (*A. karwinskii*)
- Jabalí (*A. convallis*)
- Maguey mexicano (*A. rhodacantha*)
- Papalometl (*A. potatorum*)
- Sierra negra (*A. americana* var. *oaxacensis*)
- Tepeztate (*A. marmorata*)
- Tobalá (*A. seemanniana*)

For more information on agaves, a splendid resource is *Agaves of Continental North America* by Howard Scott Gentry.

Women of Mezcal – Mezcalilleras

There was a brief time when Mexico was misguided. Oh, yes, it's true. There was a time when Mexicans blindly and stupidly followed in the steps of their American neighbors . . . and actually forbade alcohol! Prohibition of any kind usually leads to trouble, from Al Capone to Narco-Kingpins.

But I digress, as I make a sign of the cross.

Oaxaca's mezcal was spared this folly by . . . women. Isn't that always the case? Foolish men have to be rescued by sensible women.

Santa Catarina Minas enjoys the distinction of being the birthplace of the mezcalilleras, the Women of Mezcal.

Picture it: 20th century Mexico. Prohibitions of all sorts on the production and sale of distilled spirits are the law of the land. Tax inspectors sweep into towns looking for palenques, outdoor areas equipped with stills, pit ovens, and grinding stones, evidence that illicit mezcal production is taking place. Activity becomes frenzied as word spreads throughout the town. Villagers quickly disassemble their palenques. Chickens and pigs make all kind of ruckus at the sight of such human activity. You get the picture.

It was in this context—of breaking the law, evading taxes, and defending a traditional way of life—that women stepped up to the plate.

How?

Through duplicitous, dastardly, and deceitful ways. Haven't these been the reasons women were accused of witchcraft and burned at the stake for centuries?

Who cares? In Oaxaca, these *Mezcalilleras* – not to be confused with Salem witches – embarked upon a scheme.

They jerry-rigged outdoor palenques, which could be easily moved from one clandestine location to another, frustrating the infrequent arrival of tax inspectors. They set about to rotate the location where mezcal was sold—if it was Wednesday, mezcal was sold in Zimatlán de Álvarez; on Thursdays, one had to travel to Zaachila; Fridays was mezcal day in Ocotlán de Morelos; and on Sundays mezcal flowed San Pablo Huixtepec or San Pedro Apóstol, depending on the willingness of the parish priest to look the other way.

Mondays, Tuesdays, and Saturdays were the days when the women moved from town to town or were occupied with the business of distribution and administration of their business. This included shipping the flagons, made of black clay and capable of holding 40 liters [10.5 gallons] of mezcal, by donkey to the various towns. (Now as then, among villagers, mezcal is sold *por medida* – by the measure – which is defined as 5 liters, which equals 1.3 gallons.) Mothers would enter the business to sell their sons' mezcal; wives would help get their husbands' production to markets; and sisters would help their brothers evade the tax inspectors.

Of course these women have names, and are still remembered as being *mezcalilleras*

who were steadfast in defending the right of Oaxacans to continue their traditional, if inebriated, way of life. Among the legendary *mezcalilleras* still honored for their dedication to cultivating the clandestine production, distribution, and sale of mezcal are Isabel Martínez, Rosa Sánchez, and Modesta Ángeles. Above all these women stands one family, the Arellanes family, whose women—Alicia, Altagracia, Paula, and Plácia—are remembered to this day for their entrepreneurial skills.

In due course, laws were repealed and tax inspections ceased to be excuses to raid artisanal mezcal manufacturing.

Common sense prevailed: prohibition ended.

With modern innovations—highways replaced country roads, cars and trucks made transportation far easier than travel by horse or donkey—men reclaimed their traditional role in the production, distribution, and sale of mezcal. Women receded to the background, letting their husbands, brothers, and sons carry on with the family tradition. Spirit speculators, known as *acaparadores*, entered the market and today function like wholesalers and middlemen.

This is not to say that women have been excluded from the mezcal business, since they are central to its role in the life of the Oaxacan family. In the coastal region of Oaxaca, traditional songs and dances celebrate the "liberating" effect mezcal has on women, and how, rendered uninhibited by the power of this firewater, they are the sexual aggressors who fight each other over men. Throughout Oaxaca there are towns, including Yogana, where women still dominate the artisanal production of mezcal. And of course it's almost impossible to drive around Oaxaca and not see family enterprises where wives and daughters do not share the work of making, bottling, and selling mezcal. Truth be told, today most women manage the books in these family-run cottage businesses.

The spirit of the *mezcalilleras* is alive and well in the potent firewater of Oaxaca, which continues to cast an enchanting spell on those fortunate to delight in the witchcraft of Oaxaca's bewitching spirit.

The Bearers of Firewater

1

n Western mythology we honor Prometheus for having given humanity the gift of fire.

Whom do we honor for having given firewater to United States?

If we were inclined to place crowns on heads and hand out scepters, then, there is a distinct brotherhood of entrepreneurs who deserve recognition for introducing mezcal to the American market. These are five men who are at the forefront of importing mezcal from Oaxaca to the U.S.

*E*ach of these **entrepreneurs** has worked to inculcate a mezcal culture in the United States, and each remains at the forefront of the evangelization narrative of the virtues of the perfect wonder that is mezcal.

John Rexer
of Ilegal Mezcal
www.ilegalmezcal.com

Richard Betts
of Sombra
www.sombraoaxaca.com

Ignacio Carballido
of Los Amantes
www.losamantes.com

Ron Cooper
of Del Maguey
www.mezcal.com

Guillermo Olguín
of Casa Mezcal
www.casamezcalny.com

Mezcal vs. Tequila

What's the deal?

All tequilas are mezcal, but not all mezcals are tequila.

As a producer of mezcal made using only the blue agave, the town of Tequila had acquired fame by the early nineteenth century. Based on this, the Mexican government created an appellation of sorts around the area of Guadalajara and Jalisco that includes Tequila and Tepatitlan. In addition to this boundary, tequila must be made from the blue agave (the espadine Sombra uses is the genetic mother of the blue agave) and must be oven cooked (as opposed to roasted with smoke as we do with Sombra). Tequila has seen tremendous growth and success in the ultra-premium spirit segment of late, while there's been very little inspired mezcal.

Historically, most mezcal has been cheap, of poor quality, and often had a worm in the bottle. The worm, of course, was a marketing gimmick to mask the chemical taste of poorly produced mezcal. In stark contrast to this sad production is Sombra, a single-site, organically farmed, high altitude agave that is expertly distilled in the traditional method. Sombra is a testament that world-class agave spirits do exist outside of Tequila.

—Richard Betts

Mezcal in Oaxaca City

*Y*ou knew you were in for adventure. The moment the plane lifted off from Mexico City and banked south. What was that out your window? It was spewing white smoke. That much was certain. Could it have been . . . *an active volcano*?

It was. Between Mexico City and Oaxaca City lies an active volcano, billowing smoke and steam into the atmosphere.

The subsoil is hot. The Mexican earth beneath your feet is always . . . *caliente*.

That is not immediately obvious, for when you land in Oaxaca City, the first thing you notice is the cool mountain air touching your skin. The second thing you notice is the clear horizon: mountains surround you.

This much is a self-evident truth: you are in a valley, a sanctuary, a place where mezcal defines life as much as food, music, song, and dance.

These are people who live vintage lives, ordered randomness, nostalgic—yet burdened by iPhones and Twitter accounts. Men have leathered hands and women are covered in shawls. It is an arid land, with cactus used as ornamental plants, giving gardens the sensation of tranquility, a place of Zen.

Then it dawns on you: You are here for the mezcal. You are here for the perfect wonder.

You are here to dispel the distant haughtiness of D. H. Lawrence in his adventures and misadventures, his confidences and misgivings about Mexico. You are here to discard *Mornings in Mexico* for Ernest Hemingway's *The Old Man and the Sea*.

You are here for the kind of experience you wish you could bottle and hand over to your grandchildren, if only it were possible to bottle life's adventures that way. You are here to acquire the kind of wisdom that others will recognize as the decades drift by, as alluring as an engraved cigarette case or a vintage leather carrying case.

There will be stories to accompany each scar.

The first temple of mezcal is La Mezcaloteca. A cross between a library, the bar at a New York university club, and a speakeasy, this is as much a tasting bar as it is a temple devoted to the study of mezcal.

The Maestro Mezcalero is Aniceto García. He hails from Miahuatlán, Oaxaca. His mezcal is derived from the Tobala (*A. potatorum*). He bakes the agave hearts in an earthen pit oven and uses copper alembics for distillation. His mezcal is 48 percent alcohol (96 proof), and it is sold without the benefit of a commercial brand. In other words, it is only available here.

At La Mezcaloteca, mezcal is served as flights and sold by the bottle. A three-tasting flight will set you back 100 pesos ($8 USD).

Listen, taste, learn. Repeat as necessary.

Upon leaving this establishment, the cool mountain air awakens you, almost as if you had had a shot of espresso.

You then find yourself outside the Mezcalería Los Amantes, Spanish for "The Lovers." Empowered with a little knowledge, you now enter a small, tidy, and completely eclectic creation of the ingenious mind of Guillermo Olguín.

When Miguel de Cervantes (William Shakespeare's contemporary) wrote his novel, he gave it the full title *El ingenioso hidalgo don Quijote de la Mancha,* or *The Ingenious Gentleman Don Quixote of La Mancha*. I mention this because it is important to point out the Hispanic predisposition to recognize, honor, and exalt those who are ingenious.

Yes, Mezcalería Los Amantes, a labor of love, is the creation of the ingenious Guillermo Olguín, Oaxaca's adopted son. (He was born in Mexico City, for which I have absolved him, if you must know.) Olguín has worked—not unlike a man in pursuit of an impossible dream—to inculcate the culture of mezcal around the globe.

To step into Mezcalería Los Amantes is to step into an apothecary's fantasy writ large.

Calm down. No need to get too excited.

Then again, perhaps I'm mistaken. Perhaps you should get excited. Perhaps with mezcal moving through your veins, you should, like a vampire who tastes those precious red, hot drops of blood for the first time . . . *only crave more* . . .

Mezcalería Los Amantes is home to unrivaled mezcal. The sights, sounds, and aura are only possible through the collection of heirlooms, artifacts, *objets d'art*, and relics that inform the Mexican sensibilities.

Don't be surprised if a woman who looks exactly like Frida Kahlo—or is that Diana Vreeland or Charlize Theron?—enters, demanding, in a sultry voice, to be served mezcal in a small gourd.

Who needs glassware when you can have . . . authenticity?

It is said that if you are at **Mezquería Los Amantes** long enough, everyone in Oaxaca worth meeting will cram into the space over the course of the evening. Or, if you're more sensible, you can just inquire to see if León Lory or Eric Hernández, who actually are responsible for the day-to-day operations, are around. Connoisseurs extraordinaire, they are the high priests under whose guidance this temple flourishes.

What does this tell you? That amid this mezcal opulence is a place of camaraderie second to none, where you had better know a thing or two about mezcals, since people come here primarily to enjoy, not to learn.

Yes, the amenable bartender—wasn't he smoking a joint in front of the Church of Santo Domingo earlier in the evening?—will gladly share with you a slice of the maguey heart. It's still warm from the earthen pit oven. It's still aromatic. It has the taste of smokiness, of the earth from which it came. Is it the flavor of pineapple? Of sugarcane? Of forbidden fruit?

And yes, he kindly moves a small plate over to you for the fibrous remains of the maguey. Olives have their pits, and maguey—like sugarcane—has its fiber.

Once you were lost, and now you are found.

This might be a good time for an espresso or piece of dark chocolate. Anything to help prepare you for the next stop, south of Centro.

This place, called **Cuish**, is peculiar and off the beaten path. Unpretentious, it's quite possible to walk right past it and miss it. It looks more like a garage, and you expect to find half-broken men working on fully broken cars outside.

Yes, it is true: you will now have traveled from a temple of mezcal to a shrine to mezcal . . . and now to a pagan outpost in the urban wilderness of lost souls.

What is this place? There are *putas* (prostitutes) on the streets, and the rooms in the adjacent building are rented by the hour ($8 USD/hour).

Once upon a time, this would have been called a whorehouse. Today, it is a recommendation from the *New York Times*.

Who knew the Gray Lady was a slut?

This is a rhetorical question because we all know the Gray Lady has always been a slut.

That's what makes her so marvelous!

But I digress.

There's a difference between falling for you and falling to the floor. Oh, I promise you! Some gracious soul will be there to embrace you.

Yes, that's what mezcal calls out: these varietals available at Cuish will be there for you.

Its claim to fame? That it attracts visitors from the world over.

Make no mistake. When, not if, you do journey to Oaxaca, and you will journey to Oaxaca if you intend to live a life well lived, it is worth driving to the villages to see master artisans pursue their craft.

Here are six mezcal makers of such renown they have been officially recognized as Maestros in their craft by *La Unión de Productores del Tradicional Mezcal de Oaxaca, A.C.*, a nonprofit organization dedicated to recognizing excellence in artisanal mezcal traditions, and you can sample their mezcals at Cuish.

Master *Mezcalilleros* of Oaxaca showcased at Cuish

	Agave used	Town	Fermentation Process	Oven	Distilled	Alcohol Content
Jabalí *Maestro Mezcalillero* Germain Santiago	Tobaziche	Santa Catarina Minas	Natural, using wooden barrels	Earthen pit oven	Clay pots	52% (104 proof)
Tobala *Maestro Mezcalillero* Agustín Cortes García	Tobala	San Guillermo, Miahuatlán	Natural, using live oak tubs	Earthen pit oven	Copper pots	50% (100 proof)
Espadín *Maestro Mezcalillero* Clemente Hernández	Espadín	Mantecas	Natural, using wooden barrels	Earthen pit oven	Copper pots	50% (100 proof)

	Agave used	Town	Fermentation Process	Oven	Distilled	Alcohol Content
Tobaziche *Maestro Mezcalillero* Francisco García León	Tobaziche	San Guillermo, Miahutlán	Natural, using wooden barrels	Earthen pit oven	Copper pots	53% (106 proof)
Mexicano *Maestro Mezcalillero* Demetrio Vásquez	Mexicano	Santa María la Pila, Miahuatlán	Natural, using wooden barrels	Earthen pit oven	Copper pots	48% (96 proof)
Arroqueño *Maestro Mezcalillero:* Joel López Ruiz	Arroqueño	San Nicolás Bramaderos, Mihuatlán	Natural, using wooden barrels	Earthen pit oven	Copper pots	50% (100 proof)

These mezcals are sold under the cooperative's own brand, Cuish, found on the same street where Oaxaca's *putas* ply their trade.

That is the last thing you remember . . . the vision of *putas*, with very large hearts, wandering the streets under the gaze of the ubiquitous Virgin of Guadalupe, condemned to entertain some very small parts on the streets of Oaxaca.

How you got back to the Camino Real is unclear. The matter of the empty bottles and the question of banana splits delivered by room service remain a mystery.

Mezcal Crawl in Oaxaca City

Mezcaloteca
Reforma No. 506
Col. Centro
Oaxaca de Juárez
Telephone: (52) 01 951-514-0082
www.mezcaloteca.com

Mezcalería Los Amantes
Allend No.107
Col. Centro
Oaxaca de Juárez
Cell: (044) 951-136-4099
www.losamantes.com

Mezcal Cuish
Calle Díaz Ordaz No. 712
Col. Centro
Oaxaca de Juárez
Telephone: (52) 01-951-516-8791

The Mezcal in Your Spa

I'm sure that the last time you were at the Four Season resort in Punta Mita in Nayarit State you were intrigued by massage with tequila they offered. I know I was. But shouldn't there have been a warning? Rubbing flammable Mexican spirits into one's flesh? It tingles and stings and soothes and relaxes the mind as the scent and the pressure of the massage send you, if not into another dimension, at least into a more relaxed state of mind.

Up the ante. Yes, tequila is one thing . . . and mezcal is another.

This is especially true when mezcal is mixed with even more potent combustibles. What do I mean? I'm speaking of you and your partner? No doubt that rubbing mezcal into the skin of someone with a body as hot as the two of you is likely to cause an explosion, or at the very least incur the risk of spontaneous combustion.

The Victorians, sexually repressed and possessed of vivid imaginations, were enthralled by accounts of spontaneous combustion. In these stories, people burst into flames and, oftentimes, the only thing remaining, apart from an outline in ash, were their skulls and the extremities of their fingers.

How did English Victorians become so depraved? Opium? Cocaine? Absinthe?

Spontaneous combustion, everyone knows, can only happen with . . . mezcal coursing through your veins.

I'm glad you agree: there should be a warning on the label.

Now then, let's get it right. First, a warning: a massage with an oil or ointment that has been suffused with mezcal becomes a different spa experience from others in which you have partaken. There is an undeniable sensation of sensuality when a fine spirit is massaged into one's skin.

When mixed with essential oils, the combination can be exhilarating, comparable to having peppermint or eucalyptus soaps lathered all over one's self. That said, mezcal is now being used for massages at several renowned spa resorts. My recommendation? Prior to a massage, have an exfoliation treatment, preferably with cacao. For the massage itself, go for sage or rosemary essential oils suffused with mezcal.

That's when magic happens.

That's when your mind wanders off to another dimension, if only for a while. That's when you can almost combust spontaneously.

The Camino Unreal

Mother Nature, you magnificent creation!

What can I say? You've done it again.

There is a strong case to be made that with mezcal, Mother Nature rivals one of her other magnificent creations: orgasms. Yes, mezcal is that wonderful. A few swigs of a mezcal and, instantly, you'll have the *cojones* to venture forth. That Oaxacan delicacy consisting of fried grasshoppers? If I let you at them, you'll eat them as if they were salted cashews, or popcorn—if kernels of popcorn had eight crunchy legs. Mezcal may be the first spirit on earth to have gone viral. Yes! That's how it happened! Now you remember . . . You had a dream once.

Surrounded by bootleggers . . . a parade honoring the Virgin of Guadalupe . . . a jukebox blaring Mexican love songs from decades gone by, intermixed with U2, belting out *Sunday Bloody Sunday*. And a beautiful woman handed you a mezcal-laced Mary, the bloody kind, a mixed drink consisting of tomato juice, mezcal, and spices: salt, pepper, lemon, onion, horseradish, garlic. Garnished with celery, glass rimmed with coarse salt and chipotle.

Which ingredients, and in what proportions? Don't fret. Here it is:

Bloody Mezcal
1 ½ ounces of Mezcal
½ ounce of lemon juice
dash of Tabasco
dash Worcestershire
tomato juice
pinch black pepper and pinch of salt
    Prepared as a regular Bloody Mary

I now digress.

Picture a monastery. Add room service. Imagine solicitous staff willing to indulge your misguided thoughts.

Was there a knock at the door? Was it the ghost of a nun from this former, now reformed, monastery?

Was it you? Was it the mezcal? Was it a dream? Or was it a nightmare?

Is this how the Camino Real in Oaxaca City became the Camino Unreal?

There is a massage arranged. There is mezcal soothed into your skin. There is the imagery of bootleg mezcal, poured from a sumptuous black pottery vessel. There is tranquility. Hummingbirds dance from flower to flower outside your window, discernible through the white curtains.

Should there be caged canaries to warn you of impending doom should it arrive?

There is a playlist in the background, white noise that comes to the forefront. Make mine with a double shot of mezcal, you hear yourself saying.

Yes, two shots of mezcal.

Will there be mezcal in your body scrub? The facial mask? Who knows? What you do know, however, is that there will be mezcal in your veins, and your internal organs, and there will be mezcal in the scent of your urine.

There won't be regret.

You've been waiting quite a while to be able to say that: Have you forgotten? I've absolved you for whatever happens under the spell of mezcal. Yes, I fully understand not all jurisdictions accept my absolving you as diplomatic immunity. They should.

There won't be regret in a life lived under the spell of mezcal. There may be truth in wine, but there is wisdom in mezcal.

Medicinal Mezcal

Along the coastal shores of Oaxaca, on the Pacific Ocean, there is song and there are people and there is life. It contains the exuberance of youth, where the waves, coming ashore on the tropical beaches, offer a rhythm, as comforting as breathing. Traditions evolved conducive to mezcal becoming first healing, then sensual. From the tropical coast to the cool mountain plateaus of Oaxaca, the smoky aroma and seductive fragrance of mezcal disperses into the air, wafts of fragrance emanating, no different from the scent of wax candles, throughout Oaxacan homes.

Intrinsic in the emergence of mezcal is the mystic notion of well-being, of putting things that are out of ease back into ease. This healing takes several forms. Its high alcohol content made mezcal both an antiseptic used on wounds, much like rubbing alcohol is used today to disinfect. It is also used to soothe the skin, since its evaporation produced a tingly, refreshing sensation. Pregnant women rub mezcal on their abdomens. Mothers rub mezcal into their child's chest, not unlike the way vapor rubs are massaged into the chests of children who are suffering from colds. Newborns are welcomed into their communities by having mezcal placed on their lips. The devout put a shot of mezcal on an altar alongside candles and flowers, offerings to their loved ones who have passed from this life. From prenatal to postmortem, mezcal is part of the lives of people of Oaxaca.

Sexual Mezcal

What defines the space between prenatal and postmortem? Sex.

It is not difficult to imagine how women, discovering the healing power of mezcal and its inherent intimacy, further explored its sensuality. An elixir that women could rub on their bellies crept up to their breasts, and then their nipples. A fragrant liquid with the power to intoxicate was mixed with honey and then applied to lips to moisten them. Soon lovers began to use mezcal to sweeten their kisses in moments of passion and lust.

It became the practice among the indigenous women when their men returned from fishing in the Pacific Ocean or working the land, to wash their husbands' bodies, removing the scent of the sea from their hands or the dirt of the land from their feet. Mezcal found its way into the rituals of ablution, used to massage and soothe tired bodies, and to help reinvigorate them, becoming foreplay, anticipation of carnal pleasure.

In this way, mezcal fast became associated with desire and sexuality.

That fact now established, what about you and Mother Nature: when was the last time you reconnected?

Far too long ago? Thankfully, there is mezcal to help make amends. Now that you have been apprised of the long tradition of mezcal and sex, what you really need to do is spend some quality time with Mother Nature, or Aphrodite, or Venus or whatever name you wish to bestow on good, old-fashioned . . . *horniness*. Crack open a flask of mezcal, preferably from a distiller whose products are not widely distributed throughout the United States.

Why?

Because you are that special.

Yes, you are.

I know it, and you know it.

You deserve just the right kind of mezcal. The kind that will make your nipples erect and irresistible to your partner. (Who needs ice cubes when you have mezcal on hand?) The kind that will make oral sex explode like fireworks. The kind that will mix with the taste of sweat, and salt, and the pheromones that emanate from each other's nether regions to create something that, if it were to be bottled, would sell millions of flasks at Bergdorf Goodman.

From being a libation that was consumed in a social setting to becoming a liquid rubbed into a lover's body, mezcal evolved into foreplay. Yes, that's right.

In consequence, mezcal has long been associated with oral sex. Both in fellatio, which is the oral stimulation of the penis by a sexual partner; and in cunnilingus, which is the oral stimulation of the clitoris, vulva, or vagina by a partner's mouth, lips, and tongue, the pre-Hispanic sexual traditions center on the liberal use of mezcal.

San Pedro Pochutla is on the Pacific coast, a small town in the Mexican tropics, where lives are intertwined with the ocean and mezcal. In pre-Hispanic times, the primary economic activity centered on fishing. Bass, crabs, and sharks were delicacies, as was sea salt. After the arrival of the Europeans, emphasis shifted toward agriculture, with coffee and mango groves, along with subsistence farming, taking center stage. Regardless, the indigenous peoples of the region traded their seafood and produce for mezcal, and it was here that the storied tradition of mezcal and sex was first documented through culture. Yes, that's right.

In fact, the sexual healing power of mezcal is long apparent in the cultural traditions of the coastal region of Oaxaca, where dance reflects the frenzied power of this firewater in sexual seduction and desire. In San Pedro Pochutla, first settled in the 8th century C.E. by the Amatlán, Miahuatlán, and Cuatlan tribes of the Zapotec nation, women reenact dances in which they "fight" for the affection of their men, emboldened by the intoxicating spell of mezcal.

You have to admire a people who make cultural traditions from mezcal-fueled bitch fights!

Which frenzied songs of women under the spell of mezcal might appear on my playlist of music of Zapotec and Mixtec origin? "Coton," "Arriero," "Toro," and, of course, "Borracho" are traditional songs of the region. Folkloric dance that reeks of unbridled sex is yet another thing that cultural immersion has going for it, if you must know.

There, it's been said out in the open: the sexual connotation of mezcal in music and dance reflects the cultural traditions of mezcal and sex.

Regardless of gender or sexual proclivities, mezcal and sex will make you feel like Popocatepetl. What is that, you ask? That's the active volcano south of Mexico City that spews forth smoke and steam continuously. And every now and then, like a seismic orgasm, this volcano makes the earth shake and rattle.

Or perhaps is that the sexual healing taking place in your bedroom under the spell of mezcal?

You tell me.

Caveat

Take note that some uncircumcised men report discomfort, usually a burning sensation, when using mezcal in oral sex. The glans may be sensitive to mezcal's alcohol when the foreskin is retracted. Some women similarly report discomfort if mezcal is applied directly to the inner lips (labia minora) and clitoris. Everyone is different, of course, and only through experimentation with your body, and that of your partner, will each of you two (or more!) be able to determine how best mezcal can be enjoyed during oral sex. As your dear mother always advised, practice makes perfect. Practice away.

The Palate of Indulgence

Mezcal, Coffee & Chocolate

Pull up a chair and sit yourself down. I'm going to tell you something you already know, but you need to be reminded.

If mezcals reflect the flavor, scent, and smokiness of the earth in which they are crafted, then there must be complementary tastes that can be paired with each mezcal. In the same way that, for instance, various grapes grown in Oregon share a familiar flavor profile because of the soil, weather, latitude, altitudes, and environment, so do the distant varietals of grapes throughout southern France. In consequence, Oregon wines have a distinct flavor palate, as do those from southern France.

The same applies to the flavors of southern Mexico. When pairing mezcal, the two perfect complements are coffee and chocolate.

There is nothing as flavorful as a cup of strong Mexican coffee or hot Mexican chocolate spiked with mezcal. Oh, right, it's possible to overdose on caffeine, but what a way to go!

Let's forgo the notion that excess is a sin when it comes to mezcal, coffee, and chocolate.

That's like saying there's such a thing as being too cool, or too camp, or that the vibe can be too laid back. But one of the virtues of being cool and camp and laid back is that you have the luxury of being cool and camp and laid back precisely because someone else has done the research for you.

That's where I come in. I have saved you the hassle of crisscrossing Oaxaca, logging in at 2,836 miles (4,565 kilometers), and sampling 176 mezcals to present to you a selection of the best of the best. I'll do the same thing when it comes to sampling coffees and chocolates. I'll just tell you (thanks be to God the Merciful) which coffees and chocolates—that you can compare with a delectable mezca—are available in the United States.

Coffee: El Eden Organic Coffee is 100 percent Oaxaca Pluma Altura, and it is sublime. Its intense, sweet aroma and smooth flavor is perfectly paired with mezcal. Pour mezcal into an espresso, or even a strong brew of drip coffee, and you will overwhelm your senses with pure joy. This is the kind of coffee so rich, the aroma itself perks you up. The preferred way of preparing it is to pour the mezcal into the coffee or espresso cup first, then the coffee, and to stir gently. Some prefer to hyper-caffeinate the beverage by adding a touch of cacao liqueur.

Chocolate: Ki' Xocolatl Criollo Chocolate is 100 percent Criollo beans, organic. Better than bean-to-bar, this is tree-to-bar, since the artisans who make this gourmet chocolate have their own cacao groves where they grow the ingredients. What makes this chocolate so special? That it's made with 100 percent Criollo beans, first and foremost. And that it's grown among in cacao groves perfectly attended for quality control. Pour mezcal into a cup of hot chocolate, and it is like discovering something for the first time. Enjoy some of the dark chocolate with spices, and it is sure to lead to multiple orgasms.

El Eden coffee and Ki' Xocolatl are available at select gourmet shops throughout the U.S. If your favorite shop doesn't carry these products—perhaps you should be shopping elsewhere? That aside, El Eden can be ordered from www.eledencoffee.com and Ki' Xocolatl is available at select retailers throughout the U.S. To find out a retailer, visit www.mexican-chocolate.com or www.ki-xocolatl.com.

A note on Kahlúa — Here is an observation freely offered, so please take note: any drink that calls for Kahlúa can be fortified with a shot of mezcal. Ice cream can be enriched with a shot of Kahlúa and mezcal. Your sex life can become messier in all the right messiness with ice cream, Kahlúa, and mezcal. I will leave it at that.

A Marriage Made in Mexico

Like the cacao beans used to make chocolate, the maguey (agave) plant used to make mezcal was one of the most sacred in pre-Hispanic Mexico, revered in mythology and playing a key role in religious rituals.

But what chocolate and mezcal also share in common, and probably more interesting to you and to me, is that they both can get you buzzed. And they *might* just get you laid.

It was documented that Montezuma consumed goblet after goblet of the foaming beverage made from the cocoa bean before going to service his harem; there is no record of whether or not fermented maguey (pulque) also formed a part of his pre-harem routine.

Less well known is the fact that neither chocolate nor mezcal existed prior to the arrival of Europeans, who brought with them both sugarcane and stills.

Though the history of chocolate and mezcal are both recent compared with the connections that cacao and maguey have with the soul of Mesoamerica, they are tightly intertwined. Just as chocolate is quintessentially a New World product, so too is mezcal. And they go together like a marriage made in heaven.

As in all marriages, even those of divine provenance, some pairings do have their disappointments; but when things are good, they are exhilarating. The rich smoothness of chocolate can tame the heat of mezcal while adding depth and complexity to its fire and smoke. But sometimes they seem to fight each other. This is to be expected. But remember that it's still chocolate and it's still mezcal, so life is still good.

—Clay Gordon, Creator/Moderator, *TheChocolateLife.com*; Author, *Discover Chocolate*

Mezcal in the Kitchen

One attribute that distinguishes mezcal from other spirits used in cooking, such as brandy, cognac, rum, or whiskey, is that mezcal has a low sugar content. In consequence, it is ideal for flaming dishes, since it won't leave a lingering sugary taste in the final dish. Of more importance, its smokiness pairs especially well with limes in seafood, chicken and dishes that call for onions. Following are three classic dishes, one each for chicken, beef, and shrimp. There is also a recipe for a mezcal-based dipping sauce.

Mezcal Chicken

In the traditional Oaxacan kitchen, mezcal was often used to preserve chicken, since refrigeration was hard to come by in decades past. Mezcal, because of its high alcohol content, is ideally suited to tenderizing the chicken.

Ingredients
1 chicken cut into eight pieces
6 ounces mezcal
1 clove, crushed
1 bay leaf
a couple of sprigs of thyme
a couple of sprigs of oregano

teaspoon of parsley, chopped
1 small onion stuck with two cloves
water
1 pound Mexican green tomatillos, roughly chopped
1 pound nopal (cactus paddles)
1 medium onion, chopped
4 serrano chile peppers, chopped
1 tablespoon corn oil
salt
pepper

Salt and pepper the chicken. Place in a glass dish. Add a crushed clove of garlic and four ounces of mezcal. Let marinate for five hours, or refrigerate overnight.

When the chicken has sat in the marinade for five hours or been refrigerated overnight, roast or grill the nopales, chop them, and set aside.

Place the chicken, including its marinade, in a large skillet or pot. Add water to cover the chicken. Add the onion with cloves, bay leaf, and parsley. Bundle the sprigs of thyme and oregano together and toss in skillet. Bring the pot to a boil and skim. Reduce heat. Let simmer between 30 and 45 minutes, depending on the size of the chicken.

In a large skillet, add the tablespoon of corn oil and sauté the serrano chile peppers, chopped onion, and tomatillos for five minutes over a high flame. Add the nopal and 2 ounces of mezcal. Light the mezcal and sauté until the flames burn off. Skim the fat from the chicken. Add ¾ cup of the cooking liquid to the skillet, until the water reduces. Add the chicken to the skillet; salt and pepper to taste.

Serve with a side of rice or tortillas.

Mezcal Beef Medallions

In the plateaus of Oaxaca one rarely finds excellent cattle. The land is better adapted to raising chicken and pork than beef. This does not mean that mezcal and beef don't go well together. Here is a recipe for true carnivores that reflects the ascendance of mezcal in fine Mexican cooking.

Ingredients
Eight 4 ounce medallions of beef fillet
1 clove garlic, crushed
2 tablespoons olive oil
1 medium onion, chopped
2 jalapeño chilies, seeded and chopped
1 1/2 cups of tomatoes, peeled, seeded, and coarsely chopped
1/4 teaspoon thyme
1/2 cup mezcal
A few sprigs of cilantro
salt
pepper

Salt and pepper the medallions lightly. Rub in the crushed garlic as well. Heat the oil in a skillet. Sauté the medallions, searing them on both sides. Remove the medallions and set aside, covering them with foil to keep them warm. Lower the flame to medium. Add the onion and jalapeño chile peppers to the skillet. Cook until onions are translucent. Pour in the half cup of mezcal, allowing it to flame. Then add the tomatoes and thyme. Cook at high heat for about five minutes. When the liquid reduces, lower the flame. Salt and pepper to taste. Pour the sauce over the medallions. Garnish with the sprigs of cilantro.

Serve with rice or tortillas.

Mezcal Shrimp

When it comes to mezcal and seafood, most traditional recipes for ceviches call for adding mezcal with lime juice. This recipe, however, calls for flavoring the cooking oil with mezcal to give it a strong smokiness and suffuse the dish with the aroma of the mezcal.

Ingredients
6 cloves garlic, finely diced
4 whole dried red serrano chile peppers
2 pounds shrimp (with heads), or 1 ½ pound shrimp (shelled and butterflied)
1/4 cup cooking corn oil
4 ounces mezcal
1 lime
2 tablespoons chopped cilantro
salt, pepper

Heat the oil over a medium flame. Sauté the garlic until it is a golden hue. Add the serrano chile peppers and cook for about a minute. Remove from heat and strain through a sieve. Set the serrano chile peppers and garlic aside. Pour the oil back in the skillet and add the shrimp. Sauté until they turn bright pink. Add the mezcal, and let flame. When the mezcal burns off, return the garlic and serrano chile peppers. Add lime juice, cilantro, and salt and pepper to taste.

Serve with rice or tortillas.

Mezcal Dipping Sauce

As more vegetarians and vegans want to enjoy mezcal in their meals, this is a recipe for a mezcal-infused dipping sauce that can be enjoyed with vegetables, and also as a dipping sauce for chicken tenders and wings, pork dishes, and seafood (most commonly for shrimp).

Ingredients
1 cup fresh mayonnaise
1 tablespoon Dijon mustard
1 tablespoon Mexican hot habanero sauce
1 lime
2 ounces mezcal
1 tablespoon cilantro, chopped

Whisk the Dijon mustard and habanero hot sauce into the mayonnaise. Incorporate the juice of the 1 lime. Then slowly mix in the mezcal and cilantro. Taste. Add salt if necessary. Let the ingredients sit for about fifteen minutes before serving.

Mezcal Drinks

The traditional way to enjoy mezcal is to drink it straight. My recommendation is to pour mezcal into a small gourd and let it rest for a few moments. Depending on the ambient temperature, allow it to breathe, in order for the bouquet to become fully developed.

If this is the first time you are trying a particular mezcal, sip it and savor its body before you drink it.

First, let the mezcal moisten your mouth. This means that you roll a sip of it around your mouth, so it is exposed to all your taste buds. Doing so allows you to detect the smokiness of the mezcal and enjoy the slight burning sensation, along with its particular combination of tastes, from sweet to sour and bitter. Be mindful of the texture and weight of the body of the mezcal. Then aspirate the mezcal, which means you should draw a bit of air through your lips and exhale through your nose. What are its aromas? What of its body? Is there a tingly sensation in your nasal passages?

Once you are satisfied with the taste, body, and aroma of the mezcal, you can enjoy sipping it.

If you prefer to enjoy mezcal in a mixed drink, here is a favorite recipe for the classic margarita:

Spiced Mezcal Margarita

- 2 slices jalapeño
- 3/4 parts fresh lime juice
- 2 parts mezcal
- 1/2 part agave nectar
- 1/2 part Cointreau or Grand Marnier

Muddle jalapeño slices and lime juice in a glass. Add other ingredients and shake with ice. Strain into a drinking glass filled with ice. The glass should be rimmed with coarse salt or with chile-spiked salt.

In addition to the mezcal version of a classic margarita, mixologists throughout Mexico and the United States have endeavored to create a variety of drinks using mezcal. As with tequila, most recipes call for white (joven) mezcal, since aged mezcal is too precious to adulterate with other ingredients. With that caveat, here is a selection of fully accredited drinks.

Across the Border

Created by Spencer Warren

- 3/4 oz. mezcal
- 3/4 oz. lemon juice
- 3/4 oz. Benedictine
- 3/4 oz. yellow Chartreuse
- 1 slice jalapeño
- 5 dashes celery bitters

Mix jalapeño and bitters. Strain juice into metal mixing tin. Add liquor and shake over ice. Double strain. Serve up.

Barco de le Muerte (Death Boat)

Created by Gardner Dunn

- 1 1/2 oz. mezcal
- 1/2 oz. fresh lime
- 1/4 oz. agave
- 1/4 oz. orget (almond liquor)
- 2 to 3 black berries
- Hemp and maca liqueur (optional)

Shake, serve up. Add lime, half frozen. Float mezcal on top.

Bitter Smoke

Created by Tiare Olsen

- 1 oz. mescal
- 1 oz. Campari
- 1 oz. Fevertree tonic water

Pour over big chunks of ice.

Bloody Maria

Created by Aaron Seelbinder

> 2 parts mescal
> 2 parts Howie's Hot Shot

Combine mezcal and Howie's Hot Shot. Serve on the rocks and garnish with fresh veggies.

Bloody Maria Sabina

Created by Philip Ward

> 2 shots mezcal
> 3 shots tomato juice
> Tabasco sauce, to taste
> 2 dashes Worcestershire sauce
> 1 pinch of celery salt
> 1 grind of black pepper

Pour ingredients over ice in a Collins glass and stir. Garnish with celery stick. Add horseradish for an additional dimension to the drink.

Blue Corn Margarita

Created by Alexander Velez

> 1 1/2 oz. mezcal
> 1/2 organic orange liqueur
> 1 oz. Alex V. Eastern Sour
> 1/2 oz. Blue Curacao

Combine and serve in glass rimmed with Smoked Citrus Blue Corn Tortilla Salt.

Breaking the Law

Created by Greg Seider

> 1 slice cucumber
> 1 oz. mezcal
> 1 oz. Dimmi Italian cordial
> 3/4 oz. freshly squeezed lime juice
> 3/4 oz. chipotle chili infused light amber organic agave

2 dashes of Fee Brothers Peach Bitters

In a shaker, muddle 1 cucumber slice and then add mezcal, Dimmi Italian cordial, lime juice, agave syrup, and peach bitters. Shake, double strain with tea strainer, and pour into a Collins glass filled with ice. Top with soda, and garnish with grated orange zest.

Cholula

Created by Miguel Aranda

- 4 leaves basil
- 4 thin slices cucumber
- 2 thin slices poblano pepper, seeded
- 1/4 cup mezcal
- 1 tablespoon Royal Combier
- 2 teaspoons agave syrup
- 1 tablespoon freshly squeezed lime juice
- ice, as needed

In shaker, place basil, cucumber, and peppers. Using a muddler, muddle until pulverized. Add mezcal, Royal Combier, agave syrup, lime juice, and enough ice to fill a shaker. Shake vigorously. Double strain into a martini glass. Garnish with a cucumber slice and sprinkle with chipotle (optional).

Danger Zone

Created by Cameron Tessener

- 3 oz. mezcal
- 1 1/2 oz. Sharkwater
- 4 pumps Steve's Frozen Chillers Gator Bite
- MINX XXX His and Hers

Build this cocktail in a shaker filled with ice. Add mezcal, Sharkwater, and Steve's Frozen Chillers; shake, and serve on the rocks. Top with MINX XXX His and Hers. Makes 2 drinks.

El Martin

Created by Alexander Velez

- 1 1/2 oz. mezcal
- 1/2 oz. Lillet Rouge
- 1/2 oz. Aperol
- 1/2 oz. Punt e Mes
- dash Marshal Altier's Baked Apple Bitters

Stir and pour into martini glass with flamed orange peel.

The Gumption

Created by Philip Ward

    1 oz. mezcal
    1 oz. Patrón Silver tequila
    1/2 oz. Luxardo Maraschino Cherry liqueur
    dash Angostura bitters
    dash orange bitters

Stir, pour over rocks. Add twist of (and garnish with) grapefruit.

Hamilton Weeks Cocktail

Created by Simon Danger

    1 oz. mezcal
    1 oz. Amero Nonino
    1 oz. Verdrenne Le Figuier (fig liqueur)
    dash orange bitters

Combine all ingredients into mixing glass, add ice, and stir. Strain into martini glass and finish with orange zest.

Karen Newman's Spicy Cucumber Margarita*

Created by Karen Newman/Selena Ricks

    1/2 small cucumber, peeled and minced
    1 slice jalapeño pepper, seeds intact
    2 oz. mezcal
    1/2 oz. lime juice
    1/2 oz. agave nectar
    cucumber wheel for garnish

Muddle cucumber and jalapeño slice in a shaker. Add liquids and ice, shake vigorously for at least 30 seconds, double strain into a chilled glass, and garnish.

(*Altered to use mezcal in place of tequila by Selena Ricks.)

La Madama

Created by Alexander Velez

    1 oz. mezcal
    1/2 oz. Alex V. Eastern Sour

1/2 oz. St. Germain
dash Pistachio Pie Bitters
Top Mumm Champagne

Combine and serve in a champagne glass.

Los Labras

Created by Michael J. Neff

2 oz. mezcal
1 oz. Lillet Blanc
1/2 oz. fresh lime juice
1/4 ounce agave nectar
1 egg white

Shake ingredients vigorously in a mixing glass. Pour over ice into a Collins glass. Garnish with one cilantro leaf. Makes 1 drink.

Mellow

Created by Tiare Olsen

2 oz. pineapple infused mezcal
1 oz. Aperol
1/2 oz. fresh lime juice
1/2 oz. raw sugar syrup
3 dashes BT celery bitters

Shake over ice and strain into a glass filled with crushed ice. Garnish with a mezcal soaked cherry and a thin celery stick. To make mezcal soaked cherries: add fresh cherries to a jar filled with joven mezcal and soak for at least a week before use.

Mexican Train

Created by Jacob Grier

2 oz. mezcal
3/4 oz. Carpano Antica sweet vermouth
1/4 oz. green Chartreuse
5 drops mole bitters

Stir, strain, and serve up in a chilled cocktail glass.

The Milos

Created by Milos Zica

1 3/4 oz. mezcal

>   3/4 oz. Benedictine
>   1/2 oz. Amaro nonino
>   3/4 oz. dry vermouth (Dolin)
>   3 dashes of orange bitters

Stir, strain and serve.

The Nefertiti

Created by Leo Robitschek

>   1 part mezcal
>   1 part Royal Combier
>   3/4 parts lemon juice
>   3/4 parts Rothman & Winter Orchard Cherry liqueur

Shake all ingredients over ice, strain, and serve.

The New Double Cross

Created by Kyle Linden Webster

>   2 oz. mezcal
>   3/4 oz. Green Chartreuse
>   1/2 oz. fresh lime juice
>   1 bar spoon Perfect Puree ginger

Shake vigorously, and double strain into a chilled rocks glass. Garnish with a substantive lime wedge befitting the heft of the beverage.

Oaxaca Sunset

Created by Aaron Seelbinder

>   2 parts mezcal
>   1 part orange juice
>   1 part watermelon juice

Combine ingredients and ice in a small rocks glass. Garnish with a watermelon slice.

Pomegranate Cosmezcalitan

Created by Daniel Seel

>   2 parts mezcal
>   1 part Orchid Pomegranate Liqueur
>   1 part Finest Call lime juice
>   1 part Dekuyper Triple Sec
>   2 parts white cranberry juice

Shake, strain, and serve in a martini glass. Garnish with pomegranate seeds.

Spanish Cobbler

Created by Daniel Seel

    1 orange slice
    agave nectar
    2 oz. mezcal
    1 oz. Barenjager
    MINX the Erotic Vodka Cocktail

Muddle orange slice and agave nectar in a rocks glass. In a shaker, combine mezcal, Barenjager, and ice. Shake and pour over orange slice. Add ice and top with MINX the Erotic Vodka Cocktail. Garnish with fresh raspberries.

The Ward

Created by Phil Ward

    2 parts mezcal
    1/2 part Cocchi Americano
    1/2 part dry vermouth (Dolin)
    dash grapefruit bitters

Combine ingredients and pour over ice.

White Hot Sand Cocktail

Created by Maryse Chevriere

    3 to 4 fresh pineapple chunks
    2 to 3 thin slices jalapeño
    1 1/2 oz. mezcal
    1 oz. ginger beer
    lime slice, for garnish

Muddle the pineapple chunks and jalapeño with the mezcal. Add ice and shake. Strain into a cocktail glass. Top with ginger beer and garnish with lime slice. Makes one drink.

Zorrito Dorado

Created by Maxwell Britten

    2 oz. mezcal
    1 oz. yellow chartreuse
    1 large bar spoon orange marmalade
    1 orange twist

In a cocktail shaker, combine the mezcal, chartreuse, and marmalade. Fill the shaker with ice and strain through a mesh sieve into a cocktail glass. Garnish with the orange twist and serve. Makes one drink.

It needs to be mentioned that **Ilegal Mezcal** has been one of the more pioneering manufacturers of mezcal entering the U.S. market. A number of mixologists have created drinks specifically for Ilegal Mezcal. Here are a few of the Ilegal-branded drinks.

Cocktail Ilegal

Created by Michael Kelly

    1 1/2 oz. Ilegal Mezcal joven
    1/2 oz. Cointreau
    2 oz. apple cider
    1/2 oz. fresh lime juice
    3 small dashes of fresh ginger juice
    apple spear, optional, for garnish

In a cocktail shaker, combine all of the ingredients. Fill with ice and give a generous shake. Double strain into a martini glass and garnish with a spear of apple. Makes 1 drink.

Flip and Fall

Created by Tommy Klus

    1 1/2 oz. Ilegal Añejo
    3/4 oz. Carpano Antica
    3/4 oz. lemon
    3/4 oz. pumpkin pie spiced honey
    1 whole egg

Pumpkin Pie Spiced Honey: Make a 1:1 honey syrup (1 part honey, 1 part hot water), add pumpkin pie spices to taste, and let cool. Suggested: nutmeg, clove, allspice, cinnamon (lots), and ginger (a pinch).

Shake dry, shake with ice, and double strain into mason jar. Garnish with grated nutmeg and orange zest and serve with a nutmeg cookie.

An American Smuggler in the Land of Mezcal

They drank pulque on Our Lady of Guadalupe's feast day, as she was the goddess of maguey. They believed the rays of light around her were spines of the maguey.

We smuggled it just after sunset on wooden rafts made from planking and truck.

We live as fortunate foreigners and nomads, having fled because the other choice was to live within their language, their book, their predictable, poisoned, pale and anemic dream. I remember sitting in a cantina sipping a mezcal. The earthquake had been two days prior and the air was electrically charged, bringing a silence to the normal din of late afternoon. I watched the growing of a hushed procession passing toward what remained of the church. Heads bowed and moving as one, they seemed to float, all silent, facing forward so all that I could see was the parchment silhouettes of weathered profiles. They are not here, I thought. These are ghosts and saints and souls . . .

I am seeing ghosts . . .

"Where are you going, father," She asked.

"I'm not really a priest," I said.

She turned away from me and looked out the bus window. We passed cane fields, smoke rising from the earth where it had been harvested. She turned back to me. "Then why are you dressed that way?"

"Do you drink mezcal?" I said.

—John Rexler

Ilegal Activity

Created by Greg Seider

> 1 1/4 oz. Ilegal Mezcal Reposado
> 3/4 oz. Pisco 100
> 1 1/2 oz. grapefruit, cilantro, and jalapeno pepper puree
> 1/2 oz. Dimmi liqueur
> Splash soda water

Combine ingredients and serve on the rocks.

Ilegal Chocolate

Created by Aaron Seelbinder

> 2 parts Ilegal Mezcal Reposado
> 2 parts Rum Chata
> Hot cocoa
> Caramel Cream brand alcohol-infused whipped cream
> cinnamon stick

In a mug, add Ilegal Mezcal and Rum Chata. Top with hot cocoa. Garnish with Caramel Cream and a cinnamon stick.

Ilegal Fashion

Created by Daniel Seel

> 1 slice orange
> 1 cherry
> simple syrup
> sugar
> 2 oz. Ilegal Mezcal Añejo

Muddle orange slice, cherry and sugar with simple syrup in a small rocks glass. Add ice and Ilegal Mezcal.

Ilegal Garden

Created by Alexander Velez

    1 1/2 oz. Ilegal Mezcal
    1/2 oz. Organic Hibiscus Liqueur
    1/2 oz. Jasmine Liqueur
    1 1/2 oz. Alex V. Eastern Sour
    dash Lavender Spice Bitters
    Top Lemon-Lime Soda

Combine and serve over ice.

Ilegal Lemonade

Created by Chris Milligan

    1 1/2 oz. Ilegal Reposado
    1/2 oz. limoncello
    1/2 oz. lemon juice
    1/4 oz. agave syrup (1:1)
    2 oz. club soda
    1 sprig rosemary
    1 dash Regan's Orange Bitters

Combine all ingredients except club soda and rosemary in a shaker with ice, and shake for 10 seconds. Strain into an ice-filled mason jar. Top with club soda. Singe the rosemary with a lighter and extinguish in your drink. Garnish with a lemon wheel.

Oaxaca Julep

Created by Robert Haynes-Peterson

    2 oz. mint-infused Ilegal brand Añejo Mezcal (see below)
    1 tablespoon mint agave nectar simple syrup (see below)
    crushed ice
    mint leaves

Mint-infused mezcal: Wash mint leaves thoroughly and pat dry. Add about 40 mint leaves (plucked from stalks) to the bottom of a mixing bowl, then add mezcal, completely covering the mint. Let sit for 15 minutes, then remove leaves, laying them out on a sturdy paper towel. Roll and squeeze the mint extract into the mezcal.

Repeatedly dip the towel in the liquid and squeeze again to get as much mint as possible. Repeat the whole process to get the mint levels you want.

Mint agave nectar simple syrup: Combine 2 tbsp. sugar, 1/4 cup agave nectar, and 1/4 cup water in a small pan and bring just to a boil. Remove and cool. Add eight sprigs of fresh mint, cover, and chill overnight.

For the juleps: Make each julep, one at a time. Fill cup or glass with crushed ice, add one tablespoon mint agave nectar, and two oz. mint-infused mezcal. Stir rapidly with a bar spoon to frost the outside of the cup. Garnish with fresh mint.

Valentina Ilegal

Created by Aaron Seelbinder

    4 oz. Ilegal Mezcal Anejo
    2 oz. Campari
    dash of bitters
    juice of half an orange
    juice of half a lemon
    2 orange slices

In a shaker, combine Ilegal Mezcal, Campari, bitters, orange and lemon juices, and ice. Shake and serve on the rocks in a small rocks glass. Garnish with an orange wheel. Makes 2 drinks.

Mezcal Roads

Step from the car, and walk from the road. Run through the fields littered with agave. Run as dust envelopes you. Stand before the agave. Look up at the star-filled sky.

When will you know you are alive? When you prick your finger on a thorn and feel the blood flow down your palm? Are you are blinded by the headlights' glare? The existential nature of that artificial light?

Watch as the particles of dust dance in the glare as they settle back to the ground; the winds scatter your tracks in the whirl of oblivion. It's time to reflect, time to amend as you stand before the power of the agave – before the truth it reveals.

Take out a flask of mezcal from your satchel. Let it go; really let it go. Splash mezcal on your face, wiping the dust from the façade you present to the world. Unbutton your clothes; splash mezcal on your torso. Let the agave run down your body. The scent, the smokiness of the firewater, the allure of this perfect wonder surrounds you.

Step from the glare, step from yourself. Your scent has dissipated. You stand in the middle of the night, in a field surrounded by agave.

Drink! Drink life! Drink firewater! Drink!

The cool of the mountain air soothes the burning sensation that flushes your skin. Fire, firewater, wretched, wondrous mezcal. What does it mean? What does life mean? Is it killing you? There you stand, in a field off a Oaxacan road, at night, among the agave – with a flask of mezcal.

And over the sierra lies an ocean so tranquil it is called Pacific.

What else do you really need? It all comes together, the Unmeaning of the Universe.

Drink, drink from the elixir of mezcal . . .

Let the perfect wonder warm you, let it soothe you.

It is only then that you understand the Unmeaning of the Universe.